© 2020 Self Published by Tee L

Author of the Book : Manifest With Me Tee L
Book Name : Turn Your Dream On!!! Repeat.

Published by: Manifest With Me Tee L

Text Design by: Tee L

Cover Design by: Tee L

A CIP record for this book is acailable from the Library of Congress Cataloging-in-Publication Data

ISBN-13: 9780578716114

Manifest With Me Tee L
TURN YOUR DREAM ON!!! REPEAT.

Self Published By Tee L

Turn Your DREAM On!!! Repeat.

MANIFEST WITH ME TEE L

PLAYING THE LOTTERY

Thank you for puchasing this book! It is my hope that you use this technique to win and that your wins continue to increase. Winning the lottery for some may seem like luck. Well then convince yourself that you are lucky. Say it a few times a day while looking in the mirror. You have to believe it! The key is in believing... If you do not believe that you can win, and if you lack a winning attitude, then no amount of help or strategy will get you there. So if you believe that YOU CAN, then YOU WILL.

THIS IS A WORKOUT OR A RUNDOWN

In this book I will explain to you the method's that I use to make lottery predictions. Most of the time when I am playing a 3-digit or a 4-digit draw game, I use the rundown or workout method shown on the next page. I produce a mathematical equation using a combination of the numbers 3, 6, and 9.

The boxes on the next page are an example of where and how I place the numbers. Before I can make a good prediction, I must add the number 3,6, or 9 to a number that is previously drawn. This number should be placed just below the 3, 6, and 9.

3 DIGIT WORKOUT CHART

3	6	9

4 DIGIT WORKOUT CHART

3	6	9	3

PLAYING THE LOTTERY

The chart on the right has 11 numbers beside it. In the space beside number 1 is where you put the winning number from a previous draw. Then you want to keep adding the number above in each column until you reach the bottom, which is the space beside the number 11. If you did your addition correctly, the space beside the number 1 and the number 11 will have the same number in it.

LOTTERY MATH

When doing "Lottery Math", only the ones place counts. So we will only be working with single digit numbers. Even though you will do the math and it will produce a double digit, we will work with the number in the ones place only. On the next page you will see a chart that is completely filled in and I will have numbers beside it to show you the addition. I generally would not put the addition on the page, it is done in my head and then written down as a single digit under each column, going down eleven rows.

Once the chart is filled out completely, number predictions can be made going across or down. I use a method where I sometimes read around the 0's. The key to using this strategy correctly and being able to make good number predictions, will be in how well you know your state's frequency. When I say frequency I mean the REOCCURING PATTERN that hits reveal themselves within your state. Once you know this pattern you can reproduce this pattern, and that is how you will predict your numbers, that can in turn become hits.

COMPLETING A WORKOUT CHART

	3	6	9
1.			
2.			
3.			
4.			
5.			
6.			
7.			
8.			
9.			
10.			
11.			

The number that I used for this example is 7-2-6. In the column labeled as column 1, we add 3 all the way down, starting with the first number. In column 2 we add 6, and in column 3 we add 9. What you see here is what is happening, except for the fact that people usually count it out in their mind.

WHY I USE 3, 6, AND 9

It was Tesla that said, "if you only knew the magnificence of the 3,6, and 9 then you would have a key to the Universe".

I took this statement literally and I begin to do workouts using different combinations of these three numbers. I begin to see wins being revealed days in advance, and I now know that there is a pattern or a set of patterns associated with these numbers and winning the lottery. Even though there are some people that will say the lottery is totally random, I just didn't believe it.

There is too much evidence showing otherwise, and that is why I use different combinations of the numbers 3, 6, and 9 to complete my mathematical workouts.

USING LOTTERY MATH TO COMPLETE A WORKOUT CHART

	3	**6**	**9**
1.	7 +3	+6 2	6 +9
2.	10 +3	+6 8	15 +9
3.	13 +3	+6 14	24 +9
4.	16 +3	+6 20	33 +9
5.	19 +3	+6 26	42 +9
6.	22 +3	+6 32	51 +9
7.	25 +3	+6 38	60 +9
8.	28 +3	+6 44	69 +9
9.	31 +3	+6 50	78 +9
10.	34 +3	+6 56	87 +9
11.	37	+3 62	96

Column 1   *Column 2*   *Column 3*

LOTTERY MATH CONTINUED

So here is what your workout chart should actually look like with all math being done in your head. The next step is to decide how you will read the numbers in the chart. You can read them across, down, or around the 0.

LOTTERY STRATEGY

Some numbers will reproduce other numbers. So 726 as a winning number drawn **can produce** any 3 digit **or 2 digit combination** going across or down this chart. And this goes for almost all numbers that you will do a workout on. For example **085** could show up as a hit in the near future, from any set of numbers beneath 726 which includes **3-4-4, 6-0-3, 9-6-2, 2-2-1, 8-4-9, 1-0-8, and 4-6-7.**

Sometimes it will just be 2 of the 3 digits that show up. There could be a different number for the third. The more you chart and track the hits in your workouts, in your state, the more you know.

As I mentioned earlier, other ways to read the chart for a good number prediction, would be to read around the "0's". **Or you can read around any number that stands out frequently, that has the winning numbers suround it**. Use these as indicators, and you would look for these indicators by studying the number frequencies of past draws.

Let us use the "0" as the example, within this example. If 6-4-3 was the winning number produced from this chart, look at how it surrounds the 0 in the chart.

USING LOTTERY STRATEGY TO
MAKE NUMBER PREDICTIONS

3	6	9
7	2	6
0	8	5
3	[4]	4
6	0	[3]
9	[6]	2
2	2	1
5	8	0
8	4	9
1	0	8
4	6	7
7	2	6

Column 1   Column 2   Column3

WHAT IS A NUMBER FREQUENCY

You must study the frequency also known as the reoccuring pattern. It repeats itself within each passing draw. You can study this lottery frequency by going into the past and observing the results of past draws, or you can chart present day lottery draws. You can observe as they are drawn.

Each day you do a workout on the lottery numbers that are drawn. Wait for the next day's winning numbers, and then go back to look and see where it shows up in your workout. It usually takes 2 days (forward) for a workout to produce a hit. Meaning if 7-2-6 was drawn on a Monday, then the hit of 6-4-3 would not come out until Wednesday. Knowing your state's frequency is key. Which days will give an easy hit? How long before it comes out? Will there be a skip day, which is when the lottery system throws out any old number, or a repeat number that was recently drawn.

The only way for you to know this is by charting the information in a lottery journal, that way YOU CAN KNOW the NUMBER FREQUENCY.

You can also look for trigger numbers. Trigger numbers show up and box in upcoming winning numbers. I have an example of this on the next page. If you see the same numbers boxing in a hit, use this as an indicator, and you could make some easy and accurate predictions. Just look for the trigger numbers in your workout. Trigger numbers vary from state to state. And can even be a combination of numbers.

TRIGGER NUMBER EXAMPLE

3	6	9
7	2	6
0	8	5
3	4	4
6	0	3
9	6	2
2	2	1
5	8	0
8	4	9
1	0	8
4	6	7
7	2	6

Column 1   *Column 2*   *Column3*

Look at the "2's" going across the bottom of the hit (winning number), and even the 8 and 4 at the top equals 12 which would be "2".

This is what I would call TRIGGER NUMBERS. They will trigger or point to an upcoming hit.

FINDING THE NUMBER FREQUENCY

Because finding the number frequency is so very important, I have turned the remainder of this book into a 4 week Lottery Workout Journal. I am including space for you to fill in, and complete. You can do your own workouts, and I have prepared the charts for 4 weeks. There is a page for notes and your number predictions as well, and I am also adding an extra page which includes a map of the US.

This is because I have recently noticed an obvious pattern being reproduced amongst each of the lottery systems within all 50 states. Some states will have similar drawing patterns, with their numbers coinciding as exact hits with other states numbers. Sometimes they may be just one number off, and these can be used as indicators when producing your number predictions. Hopefully this information can lead you to even more wins. Let this journal be used as a guide, to help you produce your upcoming winning numbers. Complete your workouts daily. Soon you will be able to point out your states number frequency more easily.

Each week, you can follow along with me using this Lottery Workout Journal, as I will be using it to chart different state's frequencies on my Youtube Channel... TEE L Manifests GOLD.

Let Your Words and Your Actions Meet. IT WILL BE!

DATE :————————

NOTES

NOTES

DATE :_____

25

NOTES

NOTES

NOTES

DATE :_____

NOTES

DATE :_____

49

NOTES

NOTES

NOTES

DATE :_____

69

NOTES

NOTES

NOTES

NOTES

NOTES

DATE :＿＿＿＿＿＿＿＿＿＿

97

NOTES

NOTES

NOTES

NOTES

NOTES

DATE :_____

129

NOTES

NOTES

NOTES

NOTES

DATE :_____

151

NOTES

DATE :_____

159

NOTES

NOTES

NOTES

NOTES

NOTES

DATE : _____

189

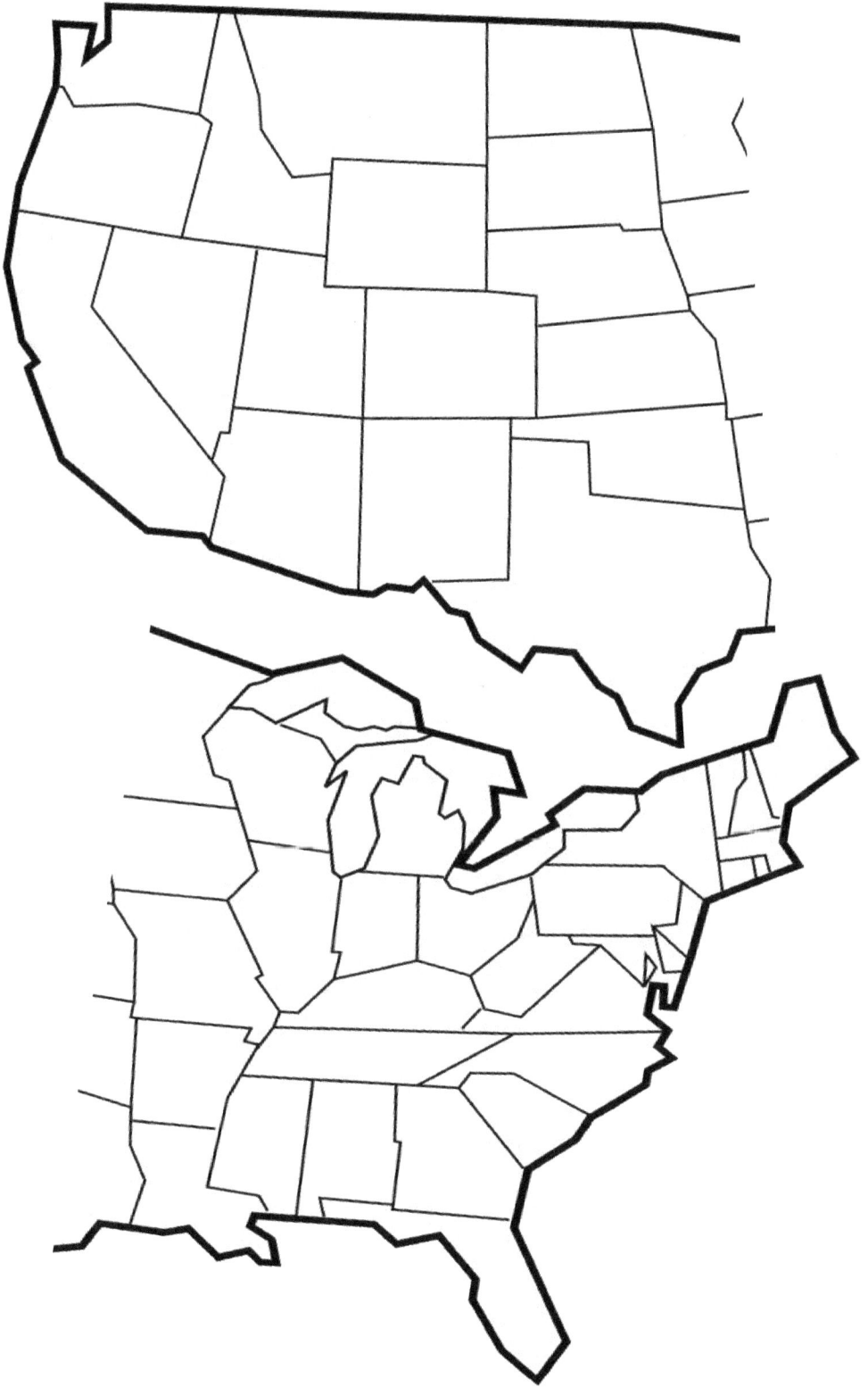

NOTES

.

www.ingramcontent.com/pod-product-compliance
Lightning Source LLC
Chambersburg PA
CBHW062010090426

42811CB00005B/807